NEW WELCOME SPEECHES

NEW WELCOME SPEECHES

by

HERSCHEL H. HOBBS

ZONDERVAN
PUBLISHING HOUSE
OF THE ZONDERVAN CORPORATION | GRAND RAPIDS, MICHIGAN 49506

To

"Cookie"

with all her "In-Loves'" love

Contents

Introduction

Speaking of leisure, William Henry Davies said, "We have no time to stand and stare." "To stand and stare" suggests, among other things, the sense of discomfort experienced by strangers among people of whom they do not feel a part. This little book is designed primarily to help remove such situations.

To make a visitor feel at home is a much-needed art. Those responsible for creating fellowship in groups are sometimes in need of help — at least in need of suggestions that will enable them to devise their own approach to meeting the need.

The response given to the writer's two previous books in this field, *Welcome Speeches* and *More Welcome Speeches,* prompted the publisher to request a third volume. *New Welcome Speeches* is the result. As with the two previous books, this little volume does not cover every possible situation. But it endeavors to anticipate typical ones so that it may lend aid in those not specifically treated. This volume seeks to strike a balance between church gatherings and other meetings. If in any way it results in reducing the "stand and stare" experiences, it will in measure have accomplished its purpose.

HERSCHEL H. HOBBS

NEW WELCOME SPEECHES

1

WELCOME TO NEW CHURCH MEMBERS

New Christians

- 1 -

It is always a sacred and happy moment when a new baby is born into the family circle. So fresh from God's hand, the baby places an aura of glory about the home. Joyce Kilmer has written of "a house that has echoed a baby's laugh." Thus he reminds us of the joy and freshness of a baby in the home.

In this moment we feel that joy and freshness, the reverence of a happy moment. We sense the aura of God's presence in this place because we are privileged to welcome into our fellowship of faith you who have for the first time publicly declared your faith in our Savior.

You are as newborn babes in the family of God. But being babies implies growth and development into adults in Christ. As babies must grow physically, mentally, and spiritually, so must you. And we with our welcome pledge our care and counsel as you continue growing in grace and knowledge of our Lord and Savior. May God bless and strengthen you in your ever-increasing quest to become the kind of children He intends you to be.

- 2 -

God has blessed us with a harvest of souls today. Before you stand these who have publicly declared that they have received Christ as their Savior.

This moment is not an afterthought of the hour. It is the climax. All the witnessing through the week, all the teaching in our homes and Sunday school have pointed to this holy moment. The prayers, hymns, anthems, and sermon have been our endeavors, pointing toward this goal. And these things have been used by the Holy Spirit to evoke the response you see before you.

We not only extend our hands in welcome to you who are new members. We clasp you to our bosoms and take you into our hearts. We have become one in Christ, and together we begin a spiritual journey as we follow on to know the Lord not only in faith but in experience. Our prayer is that we shall be worthy companions in the way.

- 3 -

Words lack the power to express the elation in our hearts over you who have come today confessing Christ as your Savior. And on behalf of all of us I welcome you into this fellowship of faith.

The word translated "fellowship" in the New Testament means sharing or having all things in common. This includes responsibility as well as privilege. The privilege of being a Christian entails the responsibility of becoming a better one. The privilege of church fellowship carries with it the responsibility of carrying your part of the load in making our church a better one in the Lord's service. In Galatians 2:9 Paul spoke of the right hands of fellowship in terms of a division of labor and responsibility.

In a sense this is your natal day, the day when you have been born from above into a new life with new responsibilities. But you must not forever dwell in this day. You must recognize that you have begun a pilgrimage with Christ. Along the way in His blessed companionship you will increase in wisdom, Christian stature, and in favor with God and man. Along the way you should look back to this hour in memory. But then you must look forward in anticipation. For no matter how much you grow in your spiritual life, the character and life of your Savior will say that *there is more beyond*.

You will come to say with Julia Ward Howe:

Don't trouble more to celebrate this natal day of mine,
But keep the grasp of fellowship which warms us more than wine.
Let us thank the lavish hand that gives world beauty to our eyes,
And bless the days that saw us young, and years that make us wise.

12

As we rejoice with you who have committed yourselves to Christ, we remind ourselves that the Christian experience is one of *being* and *becoming*. We must *be* before we can *become*. Through your faith in Christ, you *are* Christians. Henceforth you must *become* the kind of Christians God intends you to be.

The New Testament speaks of being born again and of becoming a disciple or pupil of Christ. Both of these suggest the twin ideas of *being* and *becoming*. Compared to the natural life, they speak volumes about the spiritual life.

The moment you were born you were on the way to becoming an adult. To do so you had to breathe, eat, drink, and exercise. In your spiritual experience the same is true. The breath is the Holy Spirit permeating your life. Your food and drink are the Bible and the life of Christ flowing through you. And your exercise is the service you give to God.

Likewise, as soon as you enrolled in school you became a pupil. Before you lay many years of arduous toil before you reached the milestone of graduation. But if you are to reach your full potential, you must keep on studying as long as you live.

In like manner you became Christ's pupil when through faith you enrolled in His school with Him as the teacher. And thereafter you must apply your mind and heart to learn the truth of the Bible and the fuller meaning of the Christian life. In truth, there is not in this life a time of graduation from the school of the Lord. You are always a pupil, disciple, or learner, as Christ unfolds to you new and greater meaning in His service and the life He gives.

So, welcome into this new life of faith, into this new learning experience in the deepest meaning of this life. May it ever be an experience of *being* and *becoming*. And together *being* God's children, may we ever be *becoming* the kind of children He can enable us to become.

Speaking of becoming Christians, Paul said, "We are the children of God: and if children, then heirs, heirs of God, and joint-heirs with Christ; if so be that we suffer with him, that we may be also glorified together" (Rom. 8:16, 17).

What a wonderful thing to say to you who have just made a public confession of your faith in God's Son as your Savior. He is God's Son essentially and eternally. You have become God's children through faith in Him. And as such you are a fellow-heir with Him of all that God is and has.

But lest we forget the other side of the coin, Paul adds that this heirship involves suffering as well as glory. Christ does not ask us to do anything He has not done. He suffered on earth doing God's will. And so must we. God does not seal His children in plastic bags to isolate them from the harsh realities of life. He permits us to suffer for Him, but He is with us in it. Jesus said, "In the world ye shall have tribulation [be in a tight place with seemingly no way out]: but be of good cheer [courage]; I have overcome [fully conquered] the world" (John 16:33).

But then Paul drew a balance. He concluded that "the sufferings of this present time are not worthy to be compared with the glory which shall be revealed in us" (Rom. 8:18). The word "worthy" carries the idea of scales. The glory which God gives us in heaven far outweighs the sufferings we endure on earth. And as God said to Paul, "My grace is sufficient for thee" (2 Cor. 12:9). He gives us grace to bear the trials of life and then receives us victorious in heaven.

This is the kind of assurance and life that God gives to each of His children. And as you continue to follow Him, you will find it so. God bless and use you in your Christian life!

Transfers From Other Churches

- 1 -

"Come thou with us, and we will do thee good" (Num. 10:29). These words were an invitation from Moses to his father-in-law to join with Israel in her journey through the wilderness. He had come to visit and was invited to become a part of them.

This has been our word to you. You visited us and worshiped with us. Now you have come to be a part of us. It is our intention that in your coming we will do you good. Our Lord provided the church that His people might strengthen each other in spiritual fellowship, worship, study, and mutual endeavor for the Savior.

Here you will find opportunities for all these and more. We like to think that ours is a friendly church and that the fellowship within our church family is a foretaste of heaven. All these are yours for the sharing. Since we are not a gathering of cliques, you will find an open door to the opportunity to express yourself in service for the Lord. Yes, we want to do you good.

And you will do us good also. By your coming ours will be a better, stronger church. As fresh, clean blood is to the body, so are new lives to our fellowship. So you will refresh us and challenge us to renewed endeavor in the work God has given us to do.

Therefore, we welcome you into our fellowship and into our hearts. We know that we will be blessed and pray that you will be blessed for having come.

- 2 -

The author of Hebrews reminds us of Christians' mutual responsibility one to the other: "Wherefore lift up the hands which hang down, and the feeble knees; and make straight paths for your feet, lest that which is lame be turned out of the way; but let it rather be healed" (Heb. 12:12, 13).

In other words God's people need each other. You need us and we need you. At one time or another we all have tired hands and feeble knees. If we are to be fruitful in the work and progress in the Lord's will, we must give earnest care toward each other. This is one great reason why we need the fellowship of the saints in the Holy Spirit.

We usually speak of *church membership*. But the New Testament talks about *church fellowship*. So in truth you have not transferred your membership but your fellowship. And with hearts of love we extend to you our hands of fellowship, of mutual love and endeavor. And we do so with the prayer that the Holy Spirit will ever sweeten and make vibrant our fellowship by our realization of His presence.

- 3 -

In welcoming you into our fellowship today, I know no better way than to tell the story surrounding one of the greatest and most loved of our hymns.

15

John Fawcett was called to leave a small village church in England to go to a large one in London. As the furniture was being loaded on wagons for the move, the members of the little church stood about weeping. Finally the pastor could stand it no longer; he told the men to put the furniture back into the house. He and his family would remain there. Out of this experience he wrote a hymn expressing the blessed fellowship known only to God's children.

> *Blest be the tie that binds*
> *Our hearts in Christian love;*
> *The fellowship of kindred minds*
> *Is like to that above.*
>
> *Before our Father's throne,*
> *We pour our ardent pray'rs;*
> *Our fears, our hopes, our aims are one,*
> *Our comforts and our cares.*
>
> *We share our mutual woes,*
> *Our mutual burdens bear;*
> *And often for each other flows*
> *The sympathizing tear.*
>
> *When we asunder part,*
> *It gives us inward pain;*
> *But we shall still be joined in heart,*
> *And hope to meet again.*

It is into such a blessed fellowship that we welcome you today. May God blend our hearts into one in His love.

- 4 -

Someone has said that the only unfinished chapter in the Bible is Hebrews 11. It has been called the Bible's "Westminster Abbey of Faith."

After recounting how previous people had won the victory through their faith in God, the author says, "That they without us should not be made perfect [complete]" (11:40). The picture is that of a relay race. Those who had run successfully passed the torch on to others for the next segment of the race. Now the present generation is ready to run their part of the race. And they must run successfully, for insofar as the entire race is concerned, their victory is necessary to complete what previous runners had begun.

Our church is what it is today because of the faithful labors of those who went before us. We must be as faithful in our day as they were in theirs if the overall purpose of God is to succeed. So we welcome you to carry the torch of faith with us.

Wherefore seeing we also are compassed about with so great a cloud of witnesses [successful runners, who now watch us from the stands], let us lay aside every weight, and the sin which doth so easily beset us, and let us run with patience the race that is set before us, looking unto Jesus the author and finisher of our faith; who for the joy that was set before him endured the cross, despising the shame, and is set down at the right hand of the throne of God (Heb. 12:1, 2).

2

WELCOME TO VISITORS

Worship Services

- 1 -

Many years ago John Norris wrote:

> *How fading are the joys we dote upon!*
> *Like apparitions seen and gone;*
> *But those who soonest take their flight*
> *Are the most exquisite and strong —*
> *Like angels' visits, short and bright.*

With these words of the poet we extend a hearty welcome to our visitors in this service. Your presence with us is "most exquisite" and "bright." We regret that it is so "short." And we will "dote" upon it long after this hour is gone. You are as angels or messengers of God to remind us of the fellowship that exists among all God's saints. Our own worship will be more meaningful because you are here.

If you live in this area, we invite you to become one of us in local church fellowship and service. If your visit is like the angels' visits — short and bright — we are glad to share this brief moment with you. And our prayers will go with you as you wend your way elsewhere.

But for the moment, let us forget time and space to bow together before the altar of our God. Thus we shall be one people caught up in wonder, love, and praise.

- 2 -

One of the highlights of our worship services is that time when we pause to welcome our guests. As the word implies, you are *well-come*. Your coming blesses us, and we trust that you will receive a blessing, too.

We ask that you remain seated as our people stand in your honor. Now that we are standing, the members of our church family will shake hands with those seated about them. Our expression of welcome is not a mere formality. It is personal and heartwarming.

And now we ask our guests to stand with us as we join in singing a hymn of praise to Him who has removed the wall of partition, and made us all one in Him.

- 3 -

In his *Epigraph to History* Ralph Waldo Emerson said, "There is no great and no small." This is the spirit in which we extend our welcome to you our guests. In the secular world we may be classified as small or great, rich or poor, learned or unlearned. But when we gather in worship we are one in our need to experience a sense of the presence of the Lord.

Of course, He is everywhere. But in a special way He reveals His presence to those assembled in worship. Though in one sense you are our guests, in truth we are all one in our needs before God. So with this welcome we remove the feeling of being strangers and bow before the Lord that we may receive the peculiar blessing He has for each of us. If you are a Christian, we pray that in this hour God's sustaining grace will become more evident to you as you face the week ahead. If you are not a Christian, our prayer is that you will open your heart to the saving grace of God in Christ.

Thus there will be none among us alienated from the family of God. We shall all be citizens of His divine commonwealth — and His children, dwelling in the palace of the King.

- 4 -

A college professor once said, "When I come to visit you, do not treat me like homefolks. I can be treated that way at home." Someone else said, "If you do not feel at home, I wish you were."

19

However, I am certain that the former statement does not express the feeling of our guests. And the latter certainly does not express ours. We want you to feel at home. So from the moment of this welcome throughout this service we will regard you as "homefolks" — as our very own. Our prayer is that you will feel an *at-homeness* here. But most of all we pray that we will be so dedicated to the Lord that He will feel an *at-homeness* in our presence also.

Sunday School

- 1 -

Before leaving the general assembly for our class periods, we want to tell our visitors how happy we are to have you with us. Most of you have come in response to the invitations of our people. That only demonstrates more fully our delight in your presence. If you have come without an invitation, you are nonetheless welcome. Those who came with friends will naturally go to their classes. Should you not know which class to attend, we will be happy to assist you.

Our church has many activities designed to meet the needs of the whole person and each member of the family. None is more vital than the Sunday school. Alexander Pope once wrote, "The proper study of mankind is man." In one sense this is true. But to study man in his deepest needs is to study the Bible and apply its truth to those needs. That is the purpose of our Sunday school: not merely to impart facts but to meet needs; to lead those who do not know Christ as Savior to receive Him as such; to guide Christians into a deeper understanding of and deeper commitment to God's will. It is our prayer that you will find these needs satisfied as you study the Bible with us today.

- 2 -

In a letter dated December 10, 1777, John Wesley wrote, "Though I am always in haste, I am never in a hurry." The King's business demands haste, but it must be done, not in a hurry, but thoroughly.

This thought from Wesley expresses our thought at this moment. So many things must be done in the brief span of one hour in Sunday school. But while we move in haste, we are not in such a hurry that we would not pause to welcome our visitors. Our purpose is not simply to complete a program but to minister to people.

So that we can identify our guests, will you be so kind as to lift your hand. Now let our members shake your hands. If no one shakes your hand, you shake someone's hand. And now as we have joined hands, let us join hearts as we go to our classrooms for the Bible study period.

- 3 -

In Boswell's *Life of Dr. Johnson* he quotes Samuel Johnson as saying, "I look upon every day to be lost, in which I do not make a new acquaintance."

In the light of this philosophy, this day is not lost to us. For in you our guests we have made not only new acquaintances, but new friends. And that makes this day blessed indeed.

So welcome! And thanks for making this such a wonderful day for us!

- 4 -

A mother sent her little girl off to a party with a reminder to be certain to say to the hostess upon leaving that she *enjoyed* herself very much. The dear little girl got her words mixed up. So it came out, "Mrs. Jones, I *appreciated* myself very much!"

Well, I want to say to our visitors that we hope you *appreciate* yourself very much while you are with us. And we shall *appreciate* you very much also. Your coming has made our day complete.

- 5 -

It is in Christian love that we welcome our guests today. The Bible tells us that "God is love" (1 John 4:8). Jesus told us to love one another, even as He has loved us (John 15:12). The Bible never undertakes to define this love, but it demonstrates it in a language too deep for words. So we shall not discourse about love but try to display it as we take you to our hearts.

Long ago a poet said it for us:

Love is something so divine
Description would but make it less.
'Tis what I feel, but can't define,
'Tis what I know, but can't express.

—BEILBY PORTEUS

Sunday Evening Training Session

Each Sunday evening our group gathers for an hour of intensive study of Christian doctrine and conduct, missionary work, and other matters of concern involving our Christian life and witness. We learn by doing. And in it all we have a blessed fellowship.

It is always an added blessing to have visitors. And we welcome you to share with us. Not only your presence, but your ideas and spirit will add greatly to the effectiveness of this session. May God use us all to His glory!

Ladies' Weekly Meeting

- 1 -

On this occasion it is my privilege to welcome the guests to our meeting. We are so happy that you have come. Your presence brightens our day and enhances our determination in our work.

John Milton once wrote of "Ladies, whose bright eyes rain influence." Whatever he meant by this, we want our lives to be a good influence on our church and on the Lord's work.

We have been told that we are the missionary conscience of our church. Through study, planning, and giving, we endeavor to promote missions both within our church and to the ends of the earth. Church history relates the vital place of women in missions. As in Jesus' day when a little group of women followed Him and ministered to Him out of their substance, so would we do. Someone has said that those women were the first Women's Missionary Society. And we would continue what they so nobly began.

We invite you to become one with us in this Christian undertaking. God will bless you and us, and He will make us a blessing.

- 2 -

It is my privilege to extend a brief word of welcome to the ladies who are our guests today. But let me say that its brevity in no sense lessens its sincerity.

Over two hundred years ago the poet Thomas Tickell wrote, "The sweetest garland to the sweetest maid." And that includes each of you. So if you will use your imagination you will see me toss our sweetest garland of welcome to you.

We come together for fellowship, but also for the deeper purpose of learning how we may better spread the gospel of our Lord. Not only do we study about and give to missions. We pray for our missionaries. And often one reports a signal victory in his work the very day his name is on our prayer calendar.

So we welcome you to our meeting and invite you to join in our efforts. While we like to have visitors, we are pleased even more when you cease to be a visitor and become a member of our group. We hope that you will do this today.

Men-of-the-Church Dinner

The ancient Greek Euripides said that "the company of just and righteous men is better than wealth and a rich estate." The men of our group do not claim to be just and righteous by their own merit but by the grace of God in Jesus Christ. However, we do know that our company together is better than wealth and a rich estate. And it is into such a fellowship that we welcome all of you tonight.

As much as we enjoy the company of lovely ladies, there are times when men as men like to be together. That is one reason for our quarterly dinner. But it serves other purposes as well. In our busy church life we are scattered here and there, fulfilling our duties. Here we come to know each other better. We desire to foster a oneness in Christian fellowship and love.

23

However, our purpose does not end there. As you will soon discover, our fellowship involves responsibility as well as privilege. Together we will learn about the work of our church that we may the better give ourselves to it. Information is the basis of intelligent cooperation. Through understanding, we will be able to harness the manpower of our church to accomplish that which our Lord would have us to do.

When He was on earth, Jesus gathered about Himself a small band of men, taught them, and sent them forth to work. In a lesser way we wish to be to our pastor what these men were to Jesus. We can help him carry the load and multiply his own ministry.

So in this atmosphere of fellowship full of power and purpose we gladly welcome you. We are happy that you are visitors tonight. But we trust that when we meet next month you will be with us as members.

New Church Member Class

- 1 -

As one church member to another, I extend to each of you a welcome into this opening session of our class for new church members. The purpose of this class is to enable you more quickly to learn about our church — its history, ideals, program, and purpose.

During this time we will be reading literature and having discussions about our church — and note that I said *our* church, yours as well as mine. In addition, members of our church staff will come so you can become acquainted with them and their work.

If there are things you wish to know which we do not cover, feel free to ask questions. Also you may have suggestions to make about improvements in our work. We think we have a good church but not so good that it cannot be made better. So we urge you to share with us out of your previous experiences in other churches.

In closing, let me urge you to attend all sessions. No matter how effective your life was in your previous church, you have now entered into a new experience in a new church. That it may be most rewarding for you, us, and the Lord's work, we dedicate ourselves

24

anew to understanding one another. This understanding is a two-way street — it's necessary for both you and us. So let us set forth on a new adventure in faith and fellowship.

- 2 -

Lord Byron once wrote of "happy mixtures." As we begin a series of meetings of the New Member Class in our church, I want us to start with a happy mixture. By this I mean a mixture of our lives, so we may come to know one another better.

To do this I will begin and let each one follow in turn around the room. Let each of us tell his name and address, when and where saved, the church joined, and the name of the church from which you came to this one (if that is the case). Tell us what position you occupy in daily life and something of the work you have done in other churches. [Let this be done in order.]

Now that we know something about each other, let this be our welcome to everyone in this class. After all, whether you have just become a part of this church's fellowship or have been in it for years, this is your church — *our* church. May this moment of sharing be but the beginning of the sharing which, we trust, will continue and grow deeper and richer through the years.

- 3 -

As I welcome you to this New Members Class, let me remind you that you have become a part of a great fellowship. We usually speak of church *membership,* but the New Testament speaks of church *fellowship.* It is a oneness of spirit created in us by the Holy Spirit.

John Bennett speaks of us as "fellow-travellers." If you have ever toured with a group, possibly you first met as strangers. But when the tour was over you were friends because you had shared together. That is the experience we cherish for each of us.

This same John Bennett wrote in his poem *"I Want an Epitaph":*

> *I want men to remember,*
> *When gray Death sets me free,*
> *I was a man who had many friends,*
> *And many friends had me.*

The last line is the one each of us should remember: "And many friends had me."

Now we do not anticipate that any of us will soon need an epitaph. But we should remember that we are writing ours day by day.

The way to get the most out of church fellowship is to put the most into it. This series of studies is designed to help us all to that end.

3

WELCOMES FOR SPECIAL DAYS

Homecoming Day

Homecoming Day in our church is just that. It is the coming home of those who have been away on summer vacations. During this time we go our scattered ways, some for extended periods and others for briefer ones. But we are periodically scattered nevertheless. Also on this day many former members come "home" for a visit with us to renew old ties and friendships. So we want to welcome home both our members who have been away and former ones who have returned for a visit.

While Homecoming Day is a time of happy fellowship, it is more. It marks the beginning of a more intensive program of work in our church for the coming months. Many challenging and exciting times lie before us. You will be hearing and reading about them through announcements and in our church paper.

So this moment has a twofold purpose: to extend a welcome and to exhort you concerning the work ahead. May our fellowship be sweet in the Holy Spirit. And may our forthcoming work be diligent as He leads us in the tasks which lie before us.

Civic Club Day

It is always such a joy when from time to time we have one of our local civic clubs as our special guests in the worship service. And it is my privilege on behalf of our church family to extend to you a cordial welcome. Some of you are members of our church. Nevertheless, we include you among our honored guests.

It is hardly necessary for me to recount the many helpful projects which you have fostered and carried out for the betterment of our community. But under your motto [*state the motto of the particular civic club, e.g., Rotary Club, "He profits most who serves best"; Kiwanis Club, "We build"*] you have gathered the manpower from many areas of life and harnessed it to many worthy tasks. In a very real sense you are our ally as you serve God by serving people. And our city will ever be the better because you have worked among us.

Many churches have the motto "Enter to worship; depart to serve." This motto includes all of us. So from this moment on throughout this service, we will no longer regard you as guests but as companions as we bow before the altar of God. Then we will depart for service made holy because we render it in God's name.

Library Day

One of the most effective ministries of our church is its library. But it is no more effective than the consecrated people who help us in selecting reading material for personal growth and pleasure and suggest available aids to enhance the various other programs of our church. Truly the library and its staff live for others, not for themselves. And for this unselfish service we recognize and welcome to this service the library personnel of our church.

Charles Lamb once wrote, "Books think for me." But a good book does more. It stimulates us to think for ourselves, and it guides us in the process. I believe Joseph Addison said it better. "Books are the legacies that a great genius leaves to mankind, which are delivered down from generation to generation, as presents to the posterity of those who are yet unborn." A bad book tarnishes the mind and spirit. But a good one elevates the mental processes and elates the spirits of its readers. In our library you will find only the latter. And no matter how old in years a book may be, if you have not read it, it is new to you.

We honor our library staff in this brief hour. But you will honor them more if you will frequent the library and let them serve you.

Retirees' Day

As medical science progresses, one result is increased longevity. Thus the number of retired people continues to grow. That they may not feel forgotten, our church has inaugurated what we call "Retirees' Day." It is my delight to welcome as honored guests at this service the retired people of our church and others like them.

How one regards retirement is largely a state of mind. One man said, "Well, I am *retarded* now." Another suggested retirement means the rat race is over and you have won. Looking at it from the standpoint of the wife of a retiree, it means she has twice as much husband and half as much income. From the viewpoint of the husband it may mean membership in the "Honey-Do Club." With no valid excuse to get away from home, it is "Honey do this" and "Honey do that."

Perhaps Dennis the Menace stated it for some. Explaining to his pal Joey what Mr. Wilson meant by being retired, Dennis said, "I don't know. Unless it means that he was tired yesterday and is tired again today."

Certainly one thing is true. Retirement, while it is related to age, is not confined to it. Oliver Wendell Holmes wrote to Julia Ward Howe on her seventieth birthday, "To be seventy years young is something far more cheerful and hopeful than to be forty years old."

Writing about "The Superannerated Man" Charles Lamb said, "Let me caution persons grown old in active business, not lightly, nor without weighing their own resources, to forego their customary employment all at once, for there may be danger in it." This sage advice is confirmed by medical science today.

Naturally in your retirement you are keeping in touch with friends. But you also want to keep in touch with life. The fact that you are retired does not mean that you belong to the "Who's Through Club." It simply means that you can now do things you have long wanted to do, unimpeded by the duties of employment.

Our church wants to help you to live a long, meaningful life through planned recreation and fellowship, bus trips to points of interest, and many other social activities. But more than that we want you to become a part of the church's spiritual ministry through prayer, visiting newcomers to our city, calling on the ill and lonely.

Time forbids a complete listing of such opportunities. But our church staff stands ready to help you choose work of interest to you.

God bless and use you through many years of retirement from a job but not from life.

Law Day

On "Law Day" I have the great privilege of welcoming a representative group of attorneys to our church worship service.

The late Hicks Epton of Wewoka, Oklahoma, was the prime mover in establishing such a day in the calendar of events in our nation. He spent his life in a small town, but his legal profession carried his reputation far and wide, even into international legal circles. He had such ability and dedication that the world beat a pathway to his door. His stated purpose in leading to the observance of "Law Day" was to encourage respect for and observance of law as a means whereby the social order might be a cosmos, not a chaos.

Sir Edward Coke once said, "Reason is the life of the law . . . the law, which is perfection of reason." Sir John Powell added, "Nothing is law that is not reason."

As lawyers, you belong to a noble profession — one vital to the life of our nation. Indeed, De Tocqueville in his multi-volume *Democracy in America* wrote,

> The profession of law is the only aristocratic element which can be amalgamated without violence with the natural elements of democracy, and which can be advantageously and permanently combined with them . . . I cannot believe that a republic could subsist at the present time if the influence of lawyers in public business did not increase in proportion to the power of the people.

As the slogan says, ours is a government by law, not by men. Men such as you make this slogan a reality as you interpret the law in the ordinary concourse of life, give to every man, whether guilty or innocent, his day in court, and constantly supply the oil of reason to insure the proper function of our social system.

So to you, our honored guests, we extend our thanks and pledge our prayers. May God bless, guide, and use you for the greatest benefit to the greatest number of people.

30

Law Enforcement Day

On May 10, 1847, Daniel Webster attended a dinner honoring the legal profession of a certain city. There he offered the following toast: "The law: it has honored us; may we honor it." On this same occasion, in his address he said, "Liberty exists in proportion to wholesome restraint."

It is in this spirit that we honor and welcome to this service the law enforcement officers of our city, county, and state. Like the law, you have honored us by enforcing it. And so we honor you. At times in performing your duty you may offer wholesome restraint to our liberties on behalf of the liberties of others; yet you preserve liberty for us all.

The Bible teaches that Christians should be good citizens. In Romans 13 Paul reminds us of this, saying that the institution of government is ordained of God. Furthermore, he says that those who enforce the law are a terror, not to the law-abiding, but to the lawless. Indeed, he calls such "the minister of God to thee for good." At the same time he adds that we should obey the law, not out of fear of punishment, but for conscience' sake.

Thus we are all partners in the matter of law enforcement. Your work, however faithfully performed, can be no more effective than the cooperation we give you. So again in the words of Paul, we give honor to whom honor is due. And we pledge ourselves to support you that we may have a community in which we all may live in peace and security.

May God bless and watch over you and over your loved ones as well.

Staff Appreciation Day

Too often we take for granted those who love and serve us the most — and the members of our church staff are no exception. Perhaps it is because you are always there when we need you that we have forgotten what it would be like without you.

The story is told of a wife who worked hard all day preparing her husband a meal of the food he liked the most. He ate it without saying a word. Finally, his wife asked, "Why don't you say some-

31

thing about the meal?" His reply was, "Why? There's nothing wrong with it, is there?"

I am afraid we are sometimes like this husband. When things do not go to suit us, we criticize. But when things go right, we forget to praise.

But today, when nothing is wrong, we express our love and gratitude to you. And as we welcome you as honored guests in this service, we pledge anew to you our cooperation and loyalty, that your work may be more fruitful and that it may be a labor not only of love but of ever-increasing joy.

Church Leadership Appreciation Day

Without question the most dedicated work force in the world is composed of the elected and chosen leaders in the churches. Yours is truly a labor of love, without pay and too often without praise.

This is why today is "Appreciation Day" for you. Our expression is all the more sincere because you neither expect nor request it. It may seem like carrying coals to Newcastle to welcome you to this service. If I should ask you to stand, most who are present would do so. That attests all the more to your loyalty.

In 1 Corinthians 12 Paul reminds us that all Christians are parts of the body of Christ. As each part has its function in the human body, so do we in Christ's body. Whether a part be prominent or hidden, each is important in its sphere.

This is true of the leadership of our church. By the very nature of things some serve more openly than others, but each office is vitally important. It is because you function so smoothly that the work of our church is done efficiently.

If at times we seem without appreciation, it is because we have grown accustomed to your loyal service. We do not regard this occasion as sufficing for past neglect. But it does express to some degree our gratitude. However, most of all it gives us the opportunity to pledge afresh our cooperation and prayers as you continue to lead us. As the Holy Spirit has given you places of leadership, may He grant to all the spirit of followship that together we may achieve new heights in serving our Lord.

32

Youth Appreciation Day

George Bernard Shaw once said, "Youth is a wonderful thing. It's too bad they had to waste it upon kids!" Someone else gave the sage advice, "If you want to stay young, associate with young people. If you want to die young, try to keep up with them."

In all seriousness we are happy on this day to recognize the young people of our church. While you are with us in worship Sunday after Sunday, in a special way we welcome you as a body in this service.

If we read only the newspapers we may think that young people today are a bad lot. This is because the incorrigible 5 percent are the ones who make the news. Such young people as ours, thank God, do not make such headlines. Those we see before us today are youth at its best. And speaking out of my experience, they are the finest generation of young people I have known.

The late Senator Robert S. Kerr once said that each of his children was far better than was their father at their age. The average young person today is better educated and has higher ideals than did his elders at that age. And that in spite of the fact that today's young people are the target of every kind of subversive force — more so than in any other period in history. They put their elders to shame and challenge them to be better men and women.

You young people are the products of Christian homes and the finest our church has to give. The world of tomorrow will be better because you will make it so. And that time will come sooner than you think.

Omar Khayyam reminds us of this truth in his *Rubaiyat*.

Yet Ah, that Spring should vanish with the Rose!
That Youth's sweet-scented manuscript should close!

Close it will, but only to turn the page to adulthood. However, what you are writing now will carry over to the next page. Even the pagan poet Horace prayed to his gods,

Then, gods, to reverent youth grant purity,
Grant, gods, to quiet age a peaceful end.

In other words, what you are today you will be tomorrow. The adult is being formed in the mold of youth.

That is why God's Book exhorts you, "Remember now thy Creator in the days of thy youth, while the evil days come not, nor the years draw nigh, when thou shalt say, I have no pleasure in them" (Eccles. 12:1).

Home Dedication Day

As atoms are the building blocks of the universe, so homes are the building blocks of the social order. Our nation will be no better than the homes which make up its life. For this reason our church is today observing "Home Dedication Day." And we welcome to this service all who come for this purpose.

A home is more than a house. It is composed of the people who live there. But, more specifically, a home is a spirit. It is a spirit of love for one another that stems from a shared love for God. It is a purpose that centers in the will of God. It is a Presence, as Christ is not merely the unseen Guest but present in an atmosphere in which He finds an *at-homeness*. Charles H. Spurgeon said that a Christian home should be such that should angels from heaven come to dwell there, they would not be outside their element. Indeed, such a home is but an earlier heaven.

Such a home should be one where God's Word is read daily, where prayer is regularly made, and where the family bows before the invisible altar of God.

Would you like to have such a home? If so, will you — fathers, mothers, and children — come forward and kneel about the altar and we will pray together a prayer of dedication.

> *Prayer of Dedication:* Our heavenly Father, we thank Thee that Thou art our Father, that Christ is our older Brother, and that Thy Holy Spirit is our divine Helper. As Thy children we lay ourselves upon Thine altar, and with ourselves, our homes, asking that Thou wilt not only dwell in our hearts but also in our homes. Grant that they may be lighthouses of righteousness and holy love shining abroad in this dark world. May they be as beacon lights on the shores of time, guiding wayfarers into the haven of Thy rest. In Jesus' name we pray. Amen.

Mother's Day

In Ponca City, Oklahoma, stands a statue called "The Pioneer Woman." Her clothing suggests that she is dressed, not for a fashion parade, but for hard work. With one hand she holds firmly the smaller hand of her child who walks beside her. In the other hand she holds a book clasped to her breast. It could be either a Bible or a school book. Or it could represent both. If it is a Bible, it is for the moral nurture of her child. If a school book, her education. The woman's face is lifted high, with her eyes fixed not on the ground but on the far horizon. She is a woman of courage, love, and vision.

As I study this symbol of pioneer woman I am reminded of William Cullen Bryant's words, "Oh mother of a mighty race, yet lovely in thy youthful grace!" I am reminded, too, of his prayer in "The Mother's Hymn."

> *Lord, who ordainest for mankind*
> *Benignant toils and tender cares!*
> *We thank Thee for the ties that bind*
> *The mother to the child she bears.*

In a very real sense every mother is a pioneer woman. In our day she may be called upon to bear the hardships of a wild and rugged land. But with each child the Lord gives her she explores the new land of the potential of the child. To the infant she is love and protection in a hostile world. What patience she shows as she guides her little one in his first tottering steps! She plants not only knowledge in his mind but dreams in his heart. She corrects wrongdoing and commends good deeds. Her ears are always sympathetic to the child's problems. When her child is ill, she may be up all night.

With tear-dimmed eyes of mingled joy and sorrow she sends her child off for the first day of school. Years later those same eyes are again filled with tears of mingled joy and pride as she sees him graduate from college. And as he goes to fill God's appointed place in life, her prayers follow and her love ever abounds.

The world may cast few laurels her way, but she basks in the sunshine of the world's recognition of her children. That within itself is life's way of saying to mothers, "Well done!"

This "well done" is expressed in our welcome to you on Mother's Day. And with these words we place on your heads the victor's crown. "Motherhood is, after all, woman's great and incomparable work."

35

Father's Day

Did you ever read how the flower "Forget-me-not" got its name? Whether this is factual or poetic fancy I cannot say. But the following is a beautiful thought.

> *When to the flowers so beautiful*
> *The Father gave a name,*
> *Back came a little blue-eyed one*
> *(All timidly it came);*
> *And standing at its Father's feet*
> *And gazing in His face,*
> *It said, in low and trembling tone,*
> *"Dear God, the name Thou gavest me,*
> *Alas, I have forgot!"*
> *Kindly the Father looked Him down*
> *And said, "Forget-me-not."*

—EMILY BRUCE ROELOFSON

In this little verse we may well find a parable about our earthly fathers. They are like the little flower's name — forgotten. The fact that Father's Day came long after Mother's Day makes his day seem like an afterthought. The stress that we put upon it is hardly worthy of the name.

Oh, we remember you on occasion to be sure — when there are bills to pay or toys to mend or when there's need for some extra cash. But we are driven to these remembrances by necessity more than by love. Even so, when we belatedly come to confess our erratic memory, you do not chide. We can hear you say in patient endurance like the heavenly Father, "Forget-me-not."

It is not that this one day can undo the past. But it is better to begin today than not at all. So, fathers, as we welcome you on this, your day, we remember with gratitude your strong love, abiding faith, and never-ending patience with our shortcomings. It is not by accident that our Lord chose your title to express the relationship which we as Christians bear to God. Like our heavenly Father, you too are always ready to forgive when we say that we are truly sorry. And like Him you shower upon us your bounties, whether or not we are worthy.

As the heavenly Father pities His children, so do you show mercy to us. When you have disciplined us, it has been in love. And though at the moment it may not have seemed pleasant to us, we now know that it hurt you more. You suffered with us because it was for our good. And having punished, you did not keep your anger forever, but clasped us to you in love.

So with words which come not from the poet but from deep within our hearts, we say today that we *forget-thee-not.* May God help us to be worthy children of the noble fathers whose name we bear!

Mother-in-Love's Day

Sir James George Frazier once wrote, "The awe and dread with which the untutored savage contemplates his mother-in-law are amongst the most familiar facts of anthropology." But we may well ask if modern sophisticated people have progressed beyond the "untutored savage" in this regard. With our crude humor we have built into our thinking a picture of mothers in-law which make them seem more like ogres than the wonderful people they are.

In order to apply Christian rather than pagan principles to this dear one who has suffered so much because of thoughtless humor, our church is observing what may well be a *first* among special days of the year. We call it "Mother-in-*Love* Day." And it is my privilege to welcome all mothers-in-love to this worship service.

We call you mother-in-love because we were bound to you *in love* before *in law.* Indeed, it was our love for your son or daughter and for you which led us to make the legal relationship. So it was not the law that made us love you, on the contrary, love's halo brought about the legal action.

You know, the popular practice is to eulogize mothers as though they were saints and to debase in crude, cruel humor mothers-in-law as if they were everything else but saints, forgetting that they were mothers before they could become mothers-in-law. The same person cannot be both a saint and something a little less than a demon. The fact is that mothers are not as saintly as we say they are or mothers-in-law as bad as some picture them. They are one and the same person with their shortcomings and virtues. And we love both as they are even as they do us.

You are familiar with the words "Entreat me not to leave thee, or to return from following after thee: for whither thou goest, I will go; and where thou lodgest, I will lodge: thy people shall be my people, and thy God my God."

Do you recall who said them? Not a bride to her groom or a groom to his bride. They were spoken by Ruth to Naomi, by a daughter-in-law to a mother-in-law. For in truth they were *in-loves* rather than simply *in-laws*.

So to you, our mothers-in-love, we express again our love for you and thank God for giving you to us.

Grandparents' Day

It is a wonder to me that we have been so long getting around to observing "Grandparents' Day" in our church. We have "Mother's Day," "Father's Day," "Children's Day," and days for this and that. But we have neglected "Grandparents' Day," though grandparents are some of the nicest people in the world. So on this "Grandparents' Day" I take unusual joy in speaking a word of welcome to grandfathers and grandmothers.

Those who are grandparents can understand what one man meant when he said, "Had I known what fun it is to be a grandparent, I would have skipped children altogether and started out with grandchildren."

Grandparents come in all shapes, sizes, and ages. They may or may not have gray hair, but they always have a billfold filled with pictures of the grandchildren. A grandfather is not simply the "fastest draw in the West." He is the fastest draw anywhere as he whips out his picture album. When he "slaps leather" he is not talking about a pistol holster but a billfold. However, if you are not prepared for it, his volley of words praising his grandchildren may be as deadly as bullets pouring from Billy the Kid's gun.

Grandparents have a club called *SOGPWP*. This stands for "Silly Old Grandparents With Pictures Club." Just one grandchild qualifies you for membership. Its badge is an ample supply of pictures, and the password is "grandchild." Just utter that word, and the club is called to order. Lucky is the one who beats another to the draw.

However, let me tell you something. When you are bragging about grandchildren, you are just talking to the wind. For if your listener is another grandparent he does not hear a word you say. If he is a grandparent in good standing, he is thinking of the many virtues of his own grandchildren and is just waiting for you to catch your breath in order to break in with his own volley of praise.

Yes, grandparents are wonderful people. If you do not think so, just ask any grandchild — or even parents, when a babysitter is needed. But grandparents enjoy it most of all, for they are free to spoil grandchildren all they please. They have borne the responsibility of parents, disciplining their own children when necessary. But grandchildren they just enjoy without the responsibility. Grandparents come for a few days' visit, just long enough to spoil the grandchildren, and then they move on. They get a hug from the grandchildren, and then with a hearty wave of farewell they drive away and leave to Mom and Dad the spanking necessary to bring order out of chaos in the household.

Seriously, grandparents are wonderful people. And with all our hearts we pause to honor you today.

World Day of Prayer

Tennyson once wrote,

> *More things are wrought by prayer*
> *Than this world dreams of. Wherefore, let thy voice*
> *Rise like a fountain for me night and day.*

It is in this spirit that we gather today with Christians around the world for a World Day of Prayer. And I have the joy of welcoming you to this holy convocation.

Somone said that when the world is at its worst, Christians should be at their best. We are neither called upon nor privileged to sit in the seats of worldly power or to orate in the halls of state. But each of us can lift his heart and voice in prayer to Him who is the God of history, and amid the hue and cry of men and nations guides history toward His benevolent ends.

Our Lord ever walked the road of prayer, and He urged us to pray. Paul exhorted his readers to pray without ceasing — not that through prayer we change God, but that we lay hold on His power that He might work through us. And if this is done the world around, who can tell what He can do through His people? For we are told in God's Word that "the effectual fervent prayer of a righteous man availeth much" (James 5:16).

It has been said that when life knocks us to our knees, we are in a perfect position to pray. Surely rampant evil has done the former; therefore we resort to the latter. Not only will we pray but we will give of our substance to put feet to our prayers in places we cannot go. Where we can go, we will that we may relieve the world's hurt.

Tennyson calls us not only to prayer but to work:

> *If time be heavy on thy hands,*
> *Are there no beggars at your gate,*
> *Nor any poor about your lands?*
> *Oh! teach the orphan boy to read,*
> *Or teach the orphan girl to sew.*

So today we call upon each of us to pray as we practice and practice what we pray. For this is the plan, the will of our Savior, who first set the example and calls us to follow Him in the way.

Race Relations Day

On this "Race Relations Sunday" we are privileged to have as guests a representative group of various races. We want to welcome you into our service and to our hearts.

Though as far back as the memory of man runs, racial differences have been a source of human strife, it should not necessarily be the case. When Simon Peter, a Jew, entered the home of Cornelius, a Roman, to preach the gospel, he said, "Of a truth I perceive that God is no respecter of persons" (Acts 10:34). This really says that God does not judge a person by his face. Racial distinctions appear in the face more than anywhere else. If God does not judge on this basis, neither should we.

The moral tone of our social order will never rise higher than our love and respect for one another. Herbert Spencer has said, "Morality knows nothing of geographical boundaries or distinctions of race."

A renowned writer some years ago reminded us that "after all there is but one race — humanity." The Bible teaches that all men stem from Adam and Eve. We are brothers and sisters, regardless of any surface distinctions that exist.

40

The Apostle Paul in Ephesians 2:15 says that God's redemptive purpose in Christ is "to make in himself of twain [two] one new man, so making peace." These words suggest the mathematical equation: one Jew plus one Gentile plus Christ equals two Christian brothers. Take any combination of colors, races, or national origins and the answer is the same.

So it is in the spirit of Christ and what He can do for us that we welcome you. As children of God through faith in Christ as our older Brother, we are all brothers and sisters in the spiritual family of God.

Medical Day

Periodically our church sets aside a time to recognize and honor various professions which mean so much to the well-being of our community. None is of greater significance than the day on which we welcome members of the healing profession, both doctors and nurses. None has a higher standard of professional ethics than yours. We could but wish that all others groups would emulate yours.

Of course, you are aware that Jesus is called the Great Physician. And Paul called Luke "the beloved physician" (Col. 4:14). It is possible that Luke traveled with Paul not only as an evangelist but as his personal physician. So while historically your roots run back to such Greek notables as Galen and Hippocrates, spiritually they center in Christ and in one of the noblest of His servants.

Jonathan Swift long ago said that "the best doctors in the world are Doctor Diet, Doctor Quiet, and Doctor Merryman." Well, I wouldn't know about that; it is something for you to decide. But the Bible does say that a merry heart makes a good medicine.

No group has made greater strides in this century than the medical profession. Some years ago the president of the American Medical Association said that since 1900 the knowledge of medical science had doubled five times — and that it will continue to double every five years. The result is that we live longer, happier, and more useful lives.

A fine Christian doctor once said that he did not heal, he simply cooperated with God who does the healing. Another remarked that because of his study of human anatomy it was impossible for him to

41

be an atheist. It is for reasons like this that we are willing to trust our bodies to your care.

Many years ago John Greenleaf Whittier wrote a poem *The Healer*. Of those in the healing profession he said,

> *The holiest task by Heaven decreed,*
> *An errand all divine,*
> *The burden of our common need*
> *To render less is thine.*

Children's Day

Stars in the world of drama often fear to act when the cast includes children because a child always steals the show. I feel somewhat the same at this moment, for by their presence the children have stolen the scene. Nothing I say can be so delightful as their presence here.

On this "Children's Day" it is my privilege to welcome them into this service. Perhaps the person was right who said that a child has ten thousand nerves to make him wiggle but not one to make him be still. But even your wiggling enchants us, for it is evidence of your love for life.

Carl Sandburg in "Our Prayer of Thanks" praised God "For the laughter of children who tumble barefooted and bareheaded on the summer grass." It may well be that is where these children would rather be than sitting cramped in a pew, wearing their Sunday best. But we thank you for bearing with us as we tell you how much we love you and what you mean to us.

Louisa Fletcher once wrote,

> *I wish that there were some wonderful place*
> *Called the Land of Beginning Again.*

Well, to us adults there is a land of beginning again. It is in you dear children. For in rearing you we can try to correct the mistakes of our past and point you to a better tomorrow.

Children are the dreams of yesterday, the joy of the present, and the hope of the future. And in the spirit of Jesus who once took little children on His knee and blessed them, we say, "Welcome."

Labor Day

Because of its vital place in the life of our nation, Labor Day has been set aside to honor those who work with brawn, and hands, and minds — those commonly called "the laboring man." So on this Sunday before Labor Day we extend a cordial welcome to the delegations who are present as representative of their companions in work. I can do no better than to quote some lines on "Labor" by Richard Milnes:

> *Heart of the people! Workingmen!*
> *Marrow and nerve of human powers;*
> *Who on your sturdy back sustain*
> *Through streaming time this world of ours.*

While on earth, our Lord Jesus was a working man. He was the village carpenter of Nazareth. He knew what it was like to heave and strain as He lifted heavy stones and timber, to take rightful pride in a job well done. He drew upon the lessons learned in the carpenter shop and from observing life among the common folk to teach us the eternal things of God.

Our nation is the economic giant that it is because of the complementing work of inventive genius, production management, and the hands and brains of skilled workmen. The first two would but lead into a blind alley of frustration without the third. And that third is men and women like you. We must never use our power as a nation to oppress but to serve. And we must use our skills to serve both God and man.

Sometime in the past there was discovered a document purported to be unwritten sayings of Jesus. One reads, "Raise the stone, and thou shalt find me; cleave the wood, and there am I." Whether or not this is a true saying of Jesus, it suggests His identity with honest toil. So in this spirit we emphasize our welcome with words by Henry Van Dyke:

> *This is the gospel of labour, ring it, ye bells of the kirk!*
> *The Lord of Love came down from above, to live with men who*
>   *work!*
> *This is the rose that He planted, here in the thorn-crust soil:*
> *Heaven is blest with perfect rest, but the blessing of Earth is toil.*

43

Pastor Appreciation Day

Second only to the relationship of the love of a husband and wife is that of a pastor and his people. Yet in both cases it is so often taken for granted.

The story is told of a couple who had just been married. Sitting in the car just before driving away on their honeymoon, the husband said to his bride, "Honey, I want you to know that I love you. So I am telling you now. If I ever change my mind I will let you know. Until then there is no need for me to be repeating 'I love you' every day."

Perhaps this is not a true story. If it is, then this husband did not understand human nature very well, because we are so constituted that we want to hear it over and over again.

Nevertheless, I wonder if this story is true in our relationship to our pastor and his family. When you first came to us we told you that we loved you. But haven't we tended to take it for granted since then? So to make certain that it is not, today is "Pastor Appreciation Day." And this includes your wife and children as well.

Since coming to us you have set an example in family living, deep consecration, and unstinting labor. You have punched no clock but were available any hour of day or night. You have fed our souls upon God's Word, challenged us to holy living, and led us in spiritual endeavor. Your vision has lifted our horizons of faith. You have stood by our sides in the hospital as loved ones struggled for life. You have with certain hand led us by God's grace through many valleys of deep, dark shadows. You have wept with us in sorrow, laughed with us in joy, rejoiced with us when our babies have been born, and consoled us as loved ones have slipped beyond the veil.

Through your own compassion for others you have led us to see opportunities to serve the Lord in the passing events of the day. Thus we have come to appreciate even more the words of Edwin Markham:

> *Three times I came to your friendly door;*
> *Three times my shadow was on your floor.*
> *I was the beggar with bruised feet;*
> *I was the woman you gave to eat;*
> *I was the child on the homeless street.*

Climaxing our words of appreciation is our gratitude beyond measure as by your sermons and personal witness you have led many of us to profess our faith in Jesus Christ as Savior and have deepened the faith of those who are His own. Words fail us to express the depth of our love for you and yours.

[*Read the paragraph below if a gift is being presented to the pastor.*]

Words are cheap unless they are supported by deeds. So at this time will you and your beloved companion come and stand with me. As a tangible expression of what we have tried to put into words, here is a material token of our love for you. [*Present whatever gift is chosen.*] May God give us many more happy, fruitful years together as pastor and people!

4

WELCOME TO CIVIC AFFAIRS

Groundbreaking

On this auspicious occasion in the life of our city I am happy indeed to welcome you to the groundbreaking ceremony for this new industry, [name the company], coming to our community. We also welcome this addition to the economic life of this area. The officers of [name the company] have honored us with their presence. Through their president [name] we extend the hearty hand of friendship to all.

We welcome you to a city of friendly but progressive people, a city of fine churches, schools, community relations, and recreational facilities. Your people will find it a good place to live and rear their families. You will also find here a good pool of skilled workmen with which to supply the labor needs of your factory. Your coming bespeaks a future of happy relationships. And we stand ready to assist in any way toward that end.

Of a less complicated age Thomas Read once wrote

> *The housewife's happiest season of the year,*
> *The ground, already broken by the spade—*
> *The beds, made level by the passing rake.*

In this groundbreaking ceremony we also are planting seeds — the seeds which will yield an economic harvest. But even more, they will yield a harvest of manufactured goods which will be a blessing to those who use them. Soon where we sink the silent spade into the earth, giant earthmoving machines will be digging out the foundation. After the noise of pouring concrete, the ring of steel against steel, the rhythm of singing saws and pounding hammers will be heard. It will all be music to our ears, because it will be a symphony celebrating the economic health of our city.

46

Before long we shall know this to be but the prelude to the humming of machines turning out products needed by our industrial giant of a nation. All of this is made possible through community cooperation — the leaders of our local government, the Chamber of Commerce, and countless unnamed people who have made our community attractive to our friends who have come to make themselves a part of our whole city.

And now it is my great pleasure to present to you Mr. _____, the president of [*name of company*].

[*He responds to the welcome.*]

Thank you, Mr. _____. This brings us to the real purpose of our gathering — the actual breaking of the ground. On behalf of the city, Mayor _____ will dig the first spade of dirt, followed by Mr. _____ on behalf of the company. These in turn will be followed by others selected to represent various segments of our city's life. [*These follow in order.*]

And now that we may invoke the blessings of God upon this enterprise the Reverend _____, pastor of the _____ church will lead our prayers of dedication and benediction.

Civic Club

One of the highlights of our weekly meeting is the welcoming of our visitors. Among other things the _____ Club exists for fellowship. Your presence enhances that spirit beyond measure. We ask that you withhold your applause until all have been presented.

As your name is called will each visitor stand. If you are the guest of one of our members, we also ask that he stand with you.

[*Presentation of guests.*]

Now let us give them all a hearty hand, expressing the welcome in our hearts!

Inauguration of Club Officers

Due to the nature of this occasion, a welcome is in order for the officers-elect who will be inaugurated today.

Wherever men live in an orderly society, there must be leaders as well as followers. Because you have proved to be good followers, our club membership has chosen you to be its leaders in the coming year. We have not elected you simply to honor you, but because you have proved honorable, we have placed upon you a trust.

Words of praise for you are unnecessary. We have praised you by choosing you for your office. And by your deeds you will prove worthy of this trust.

> *On wings of deeds the soul must mount!*
> *When we are summoned from afar,*
> *Ourselves, and not our words, will count—*
> *Not what we said, but what we are!*
>
> —WILLIAM WINTER

As the names of our new officers are called, will you stand and remain standing. [*Call out names of officers.*] And now as you stand before us we pledge to you our "followship" to match your leadership. None of you has an unimportant position. It will be great or small as you make it so. Thus we charge you to be faithful to the utmost degree of your ability, so that when one year from now you pass the torch to other hands our club will be stronger, better, and more effective in service than it is today.

> *To every life there comes a time supreme;*
> *One day, one night, one morning, or one noon,*
> *One freighted hour, one moment opportune,*
> *One rift through which sublime fulfilments gleam.*
>
> —MARY ASHLEY TOWNSEND

For you that time is now!

Will all of you now stand as a pledge of your cooperation as our member, the Reverend _____, leads us in a prayer of dedication.

Inauguration of Public Official

My fellow-citizens, welcome to this inaugural ceremony! It is an occasion of great importance to our city / state / nation, for we are here to inaugurate the Honorable _____ as [*name of office*], the office to which he has been elected by you and others whom you represent.

In his letter of acceptance for the nomination for governor of New York, Grover Cleveland wrote, "Public officers are the servants and agents of the people, to execute the laws which the people have made." Later in his inaugural address as president of the United States he said, "Your every voter, as sure as your chief magistrate, exercises a public trust." Thus out of the past comes this mandate to both the elected and the electors.

We are indebted to the great Pericles of Greece's Golden Age for the reminder that "in election to public offices we consider neither class nor rank, but each man is preferred according to his virtue or to the esteem in which he is held for some special excellence."

There is an oft-quoted poem which never goes out of style:

> *God, give us men! A time like this demands*
> *Strong minds, great hearts, true faith, and ready hands;*
> *Men whom the lust of office does not kill;*
> *Men whom the spoils of office cannot buy;*
> *Men who possess opinions and a will;*
> *Men who have honor; men who will not lie;*
> *Men who can stand before a demagogue*
> *And damn his treacherous flatteries without winking;*
> *Tall men sun-crowned, who live above the fog*
> *In public duty and private thinking.*

> —JOSIAH HOLLAND

We strongly believe that we are inaugurating such a person today. Yet he is human and will make mistakes. He who tries, at times will err. We must pray for him and hold him up, knowing that he is a man of like passions such as we are. Our only expectation and hope is that at the end of his term of office he will be able to say in the last words ever spoken by Grover Cleveland, "I have tried so hard to do the right."

And now the oath of office will be administered by the Honorable _____, [*name of his office*].

[*Oath administered.*]

To invoke the blessings of God upon our new [*name of office*], the Reverend _____ will lead us in prayer.

Chamber of Commerce

Welcome to the weekly luncheon of our Chamber of Commerce! And a special welcome to our guests!

In our various businesses we may find ourselves in competition. But we are united in our efforts and purpose to build a stronger cultural, economic, and spiritual community, for free enterprise thrives upon both competition and cooperation.

The history of our organization dates almost simultaneously with the founding of our city. And history reveals that it has played a vital part in the growth of our city from a small village to a giant municipality. Deliberately we have worked to bring into our economic life businesses which were to be competitors of those already here. It has been to the profit of all, for where monopoly creates stagnation, competition encourages new life and zest.

Our chamber serves for the good of all. What you see here today is a time of fellowship and inspiration. But through organized committee work we touch every phase of the city's life. We are able to bring together the best minds of the community for a cross-fertilization of ideas in planning worthy purposes and programs, looking toward the future development of our city.

And as one among thousands of such groups throughout the land, we serve to keep our nation strong. An unknown poet has said,

> *No foe dare molest, where in union are join'd*
> *The plough, loom, and chisel, with commerce combined.*

Actually foes have dared to molest our nation in the past. But none has successfully done so. The greatest challenge our nation has ever faced before molesting foes was in the early months of World War II. The production of ships and armaments during that time has never been equaled in history. But this was not done in a day. It was the fruit of many years of planned cooperation by groups such as ours which produced the necessary technical know-how and capacity.

If commerce and industry have made our nation strong, they can also keep it strong. It is to this end that we are and ever shall be dedicated.

Let me take this moment to extend a welcome to our guests. Someone has facetiously described a Chamber of Commerce as a group of
businessmen who meet and eat, applaud a message against the en-
croachments of big government upon free enterprise, and then ad-
journ into committee meetings to plan how to get federal funds for
local projects.

However, you will not find such an attitude here. We believe there
should be cooperation between business and government, but neither
should dominate the other.

Over a century ago a Frenchman said,

> In the matter of commerce, encouragement does not mean pro-
> tection. . . . Manufacturing industry depends solely on itself,
> competition is its life. Protect it, and it goes to sleep; it dies
> from monopoly as well as from the tariff. The nation that suc-
> ceeds in making all other nations its vassals will be the one
> which first proclaims commercial liberty; it will have enough
> manufacturing power to supply its productions at a cheaper price
> than those of its rivals.

Now our nation has no desire to make others its "vassals." But as
businessmen we want to compete in the open market at home and
abroad on equal terms with other nations. This is one reason for
our existence as a Chamber of Commerce. It is to this end that we
are dedicated.

- 3 -

Welcome to our gathering! And a double welcome to our visitors!

The story is told about two dim-witted men who went deer hunting.
Having killed a deer, they were dragging it back to their car, pulling
it by its hind legs. But they were having a hard time since its
antlers kept getting caught on bushes and other undergrowth. A
passerby, seeing their problem, said, "Hey, fellows, it'll be easier if
you pull it by the antlers." So they started doing it. Finally one of
them said, "You know, it is easier." To which the other replied,
"Yes, but we're getting farther away from the car all the time."

Now our Chamber of Commerce may encounter problems. But at
least we are not like those men. We know where we want to go.
And we are moving in that direction. We invite all of you to go
along with us.

Christmas Tree Lighting

One of the happiest times of the year is the occasion of lighting the community Christmas tree. And we welcome each of you to join in this delightful moment.

Amy Lowell, writing about her beloved New England, said,

> *The sight of a white church above thin trees in a city square*
> *Amazes my eyes as though it were the Parthenon.*

We may not have such a church in the city square. But annually in our civic center we have a beautifully lighted Christmas tree which reminds us of more than the pagan ruins of the glory of an age forever gone. It speaks of the event of the ages when God came to dwell among men.

Cynics like to remind us of the pagan origin of the Christmas tree. But this does not lessen the glory of the message it portrays to our eyes and hearts today. Joyce Kilmer was right in saying that "only God can make a tree."

Ogden Nash, in his "Song of the Open Road," has written a parody on Kilmer's opening lines:

> *I think that I shall never see*
> *A billboard lovely as a tree.*
> *Perhaps, unless the billboards fall,*
> *I'll never see a tree at all.*

In his wit he has penned a lesson for this season. The "billboards" hawking their wares at Christmas tend to mute the real meaning of this blessed time of year. But this lovely tree, standing amidst the center of trade, points us to the real meaning of Christmas. It stands as a light in the darkness. Its beauty for the moment causes us to forget the sordid. And its cheer emits a warmth so much needed by cold hearts.

Crowning this tree is a star which symbolizes another star, His star, which guides the wise to a home in Bethlehem, there to find the eternal in time, omnipotence in the tiny body of a baby, the all-wise in a child, God in a cradle. The rough wood of this tree points to a cross on a hill.

This tree will shortly fade away, but its message will continue to shine forth that those walking in darkness may see the Light; in eyes grown dull with hopelessness can sparkle its gleam of hope.

Only God can make a tree. And only He can set the joybells of salvation ringing in our hearts. So as the switch is thrown to cause this tree to burst into a glorious light, may God's power in His Son shine in our hearts and by reflection make us as the light of the world.

Christmas is a time for children. So may we all become as little children in the spirit of Ogden Nash's "A Carol for Children."

Yours be the genial holly wreaths,
The stockings and the tree;
An aged world to you bequeaths
Its own forgotten glee.

God rest you, merry Innocents,
While innocence endures.
A sweeter Christmas than we to ours
May you bequeath to yours.

Arbor Day

An annual affair in our community is the observance of Arbor Day. As the name implies, it is a time when we plant trees. The one tree we shall plant here is but symbolic of hundreds we shall plant as individuals. So we welcome you to this ceremonial planting, which will be followed by others as we disperse throughout the area.

Francis Bacon tells us that on this earth "God Almighty first planted a garden." It was a paradise into which He placed our first parents. Revelation 22 pictures heaven as such a paradise restored. Conversely Lord Byron reminds us that we should take care as to the kind of trees we plant, whether in the ground or in our lives.

The thorns which I have reap'd are of the tree I planted;
they have torn me, and I bleed.
I should have known what fruit would spring from such
a seed.

A tree may be planted in a moment, but it takes a lifetime to grow to maturity. So planting a tree is an act of unselfishness, for we plant for the future. Yet it is a debt that we owe to the past, for others planted trees which we enjoy and use today. The shades of today spring from the seeds of yesterday.

Failure to plant where we have hewn is to squander our natural resources of soil, wood, and air. To do so is to play the truant and to rob generations yet unborn. Time takes its toll. As Carl Linnaeus said two centuries ago, "If a tree dies, plant another in its place."

Thus we replenish our forests not by chance but by purpose. It is a purpose which cooperates with God, who alone can make a tree; and yet the planted tree is to the planter a monument that he passed that way. We may not be able to perform great deeds which will astound men. But each of us can plant a tree in the ground.

This planting is a parallel to the words of Ellen H. Underwood:

> *The bread that bringeth strength I want to give,*
> *The water pure that bids the thirsty live;*
> *I want to help the fainting day by day;*
> *I'm sure I shall not pass again this way.*

Dedication of School

Someone once wrote,

> *Better build schoolrooms for "the boy"*
> *Than cells and gibbets for "the man."*

That is another way of saying that an investment in a school is an investment in the future — and all for the good. So on the occasion of the dedication of this new school building, it is my delight to welcome all of you. This welcome is especially for the children and the teachers who will use these facilities for their intended purpose. For, after all, this is just so much brick and mortar, steel and stone. It is but the tool through which to produce the finished product — boys and girls who are better equipped to fill their places in life. Even elementary education determines the direction in which the men and women of tomorrow will go.

James M. Barrie spoke of the greatness of Scotland as being rooted in the poor, proud homes which resolved that "There shall be education in this land." It is no wonder, then, that in our own land, history records that one of the first institutions to be established in every new settlement was a school. If schools are important in lands other than democracies, they are doubly so in lands where the governed are the governors. The free use of the franchise demands education, else the ones exercising it may weld their own chains of slavery.

Who can today measure the fruit of the institution we dedicate? Those who teach here should ever be aware of the fact that they are affecting eternity. You can never know where your influence ceases. Before long the boys and girls who will pass through this building will be homemakers, professional people, even filling the halls of state. So what we do here today casts its long shadow over the ever-unfolding tomorrows.

The story is told of a certain educator who tipped his hat to every boy he met. When asked why, he replied, "I never know when I may be tipping my hat to a future President of the United States."

So as we dedicate this building may we dedicate ourselves, for the use we make of it will shape the future. Who can say what molds of character and mind are being formed here? To the end, therefore, that this may be not simply a building but a means of blessing, we dedicate it to the service of our city, state, and nation — yes, of all mankind.

Dedication of Park

Denis McCarthy, in the poem "Give Them a Place to Play," said of children,

> Give them a chance—if you stint them now,
> tomorrow you'll have to pay
> A larger bill for a darker ill.

This is one of many reasons we are today dedicating this beautiful park — that our children may have a wholesome place in which to grow and develop into the kind of citizens they have the right to become. We welcome each of you to this happy occasion.

What is a park? It is an oasis in a desert of steel and stone. It is an island in an ocean of concrete. It is a haven from the jungle of the city's hurrying life. A park is a place where children romp and play, where lovers stroll hand in hand, where busy adults may find a retreat from the pressures of the day and where the elderly may sit and bask in the sun.

What is a park? It is trees, birds, flowers, and the rippling music of flowing streams. It is a carpet of green to soothe jangled nerves, a refuge from the hue and cry of milling throngs, a place to rest, to meditate, to dream.

What is a park? It is a later Eden, where in the cool of the shade man's soul may commune with God and from which we may go — strengthened and refreshed — to meet the duties of the day.

What Thomas Brown once wrote of a garden we can say of this park.

> *A Garden is a lovesome thing, God wot!*
> > *Rose plot,*
> > *Fringed pool,*
> > *Ferned grot—*
> > *The veriest school*
> > *Of peace; and yet the fool*
> *Contends that God is not—*
> *Not God! in Gardens! when the eve is cool?*
> *Nay, but I have a sign:*
> *'Tis very sure God walks in mine.*

Fourth of July

Sadly for many years in our nation a spirit of indifference prevailed as to patriotism and the price paid by our forefathers for the freedoms we take for granted. Happily in recent years there has been a rebirth that must be of the realization that eternal vigilance is the price that must be paid for the preservation of liberty. So it is my privilege to welcome you to this Fourth of July celebration.

Benjamin Franklin once wrote words we desperately need to heed today. "They that can give up essential liberty to obtain a little temporary safety deserve neither liberty nor safety." If for the doles handed out by a paternalistic state we surrender the rights of free men, we are no wiser or better than Esau, who sold his birthright for a mess of pottage.

Ours is not a perfect land. But it is the best of all lands. Never does a true-hearted citizen of our nation return from foreign soil but that he wants to fall down and kiss the ground of this blessed land. To such there is no more beautiful view than to see "Old Glory" waving in the breeze. This is especially true if it waves over an embassy in a land where freedom is unknown, for it symbolizes a small island of liberty in an ocean of oppression. Such a heart does not sneer but cheers and thrills to the words,

56

Hats off!
Along the street there comes
A blare of bugles, a ruffle of drums,
A flash of color beneath the sky:
Hats off!
The flag is passing by.

—HENRY H. BENNETT

This is a day of commemoration, a time to remember and honor those who pledged — and gave — their fortunes, lives, and sacred honor to give us our freedom and those upon a thousand battlefields who paid the last measure of devotion to defend it. Thus we sing with new appreciation,

Hail, Columbia! happy land!
Hail, ye heroes! heaven-born band!
Who fought and bled in Freedom's cause,
And when the storm of war was gone,
Enjoyed the peace your valor won.
Let independence be our boast,
Ever mindful what it cost;
Ever grateful for the prize,
Let its altar reach the skies!

—JOSEPH HOPKINSON

But this is also a day of consecration, because upon us falls the lot to preserve and pass on to other generations yet unborn the blessed nation that is ours. Not to marching armies alone, or to statesmen, but to each of us comes the call out of the past to bequeath to the future, free from the soiled hands of tyranny, the land of the free and the home of the brave. We must remember that no man is really free until all men are free. This is true in our nation itself where freedom and right are not the enjoyments of the few, but the privileges of all.

Therefore, lifting our eyes toward the sun which moves unfettered through the skies, let us dedicate ourselves in the words of an ode set to music and first sung at a freedom festival in Boston on July 4, 1803.

By yon orbit of living light,
Swear to guard your native right;
Sooner let it cease to shine,
Than your liberties resign.

—AUTHOR UNKNOWN

Dedication of Historical Museum

Abram Joseph Ryan once wrote, "A land without ruins is a land without memories — a land without memories is a land without history." The ruins may bring back memories of the changing tides of battle or of the erosion of time. But in either case they are silent reminders of the history of a people. It may be added that a people which does not remember and revere its past hardly deserves its present or future. As a traveler often must pause to review where he has come from in order to know where he is going, so a nation should take note of its past to chart its future correctly.

It is to this end that we are here today to dedicate this historical museum. We extend a hearty welcome to you all!

This museum is itself a constant reminder of the pioneer and self-sufficient spirit of our forefathers who forged this nation out of a wilderness. While this building will house the things with which they toiled, it is also the abode of the spirit in which they labored. In the final analysis history is made by people, not by things. So in the words of Walt Whitman we salute the noble souls of yesterday:

Through the battle, through defeat, moving yet and never stopping,
Pioneers! O pioneers!

However, this museum is for more than housing memories. It is for inspiring visions as well. The Bible speaks of old men dreaming dreams but young men having visions. You young people must remember that today's old men were once young, and sooner than you think you will be the old men dreaming dreams. What kind of dreams they will be depends upon the visions you now have and how well you pursue them.

There is a difference between visionary people and people of vision. Visionary people build dream castles in the air. People of vision make them realities upon earth. Visionary people will spin tales about what has been. People of vision will hammer out what is to be so that if a thousand years from now men should gather the artifacts of today, they could say, "They did well with what they had."

Over the entrance to one of the government buildings in Washington is the inscription "The Past Is But Prologue." Seeing it from a taxi window a man asked the driver what it meant. He replied, "Brother, you ain't seen nothing yet!" We may not approve of his grammar, but we admire his spirit. And it is in that spirit that we dedicate this historical museum today.

58

5

INTRODUCTION OF SPEAKERS

[A word of caution is in order at this point. The introduction of speakers should never be lengthy. The audience came to hear the speaker, not to hear about him. As for the speaker himself, speaking from personal experience, when the presiding officer goes into lengthy detail it seems as if he thinks the speaker does not have too much to present and is trying to prop *it up. An introduction should include enough information to show that the speaker is qualified to handle his chosen subject. Other personal matters should be kept to a minimum unless deemed otherwise. Clean humor may be used on occasion but must always be in good taste.]*

President of the United States

Ladies and gentlemen, the President of the United States!

Governor of a State

In one's own state: Ladies and gentlemen, the governor of the state of _____!

In another state: Ladies and gentlemen, we are honored to have as our speaker the governor of one of our sister states, the Honorable _____, governor of the state of _____.

Mayor of a City

In one's own city: We are honored to have as our speaker today the chief elected officer of our city. Ladies and gentlemen, the Honorable _____, mayor of _____.

In another city: We are privileged to have as our speaker today the mayor of one of the great cities of our nation. Ladies and gentlemen, the Honorable _____, mayor of _____.

United States Senator

- 1 -

From one's own state: Our state has given many distinguished men and women to the service of our nation. Such is our speaker today. He is especially qualified to speak on the theme of this meeting [*name the theme*] since he serves as chairman/member of the Senate _____ Committee. Ladies and gentlemen, the Honorable _____, United States senator.

- 2 -

From another state: The theme of our gathering is _____. And as chairman/member of the Senate _____ Committee, none is more versed in this field than our speaker of the hour. Ladies and gentlemen, I am honored to present to you the Honorable _____, United States senator from _____.

Congressman

- 1 -

From one's own state: Our speaker today has distinguished himself in the service of our state and nation. He has honored us and his office through his ability and dedication. As chairman/member of the House Committee on _____ he is thoroughly qualified to speak on the theme of our meeting/convention [*name the theme*]. Therefore, it is my joy and privilege to present to you the Honorable _____, United States congressman from the _____ district of our state.

From another state: When your program committee chose the theme of this meeting/convention, it sought the one it considered best qualified to speak on it. My fellow delegates, may I present to you the Honorable ⎯⎯⎯⎯⎯, member of the United States House of Representatives from ⎯⎯⎯⎯⎯.

Judge

The very term "judge" implies discernment, fairness, and wisdom. Through his eminent career as an attorney and his long, distinguished service on the bench, our speaker today has shown himself qualified to be known by these virtues. Your Honor, we *sit* expectantly before you, but we hope we will never have to *stand* before you.

Ladies and gentlemen, the Honorable ⎯⎯⎯⎯⎯, [*name type of court*] judge.

Chief of Police or Sheriff

The safety of a community is no greater than the men who curb lawbreakers and enforce the laws of the land. But the observance of "Law Enforcement Day" is to remind us of the part each of us must play if the legal process is to be effective.

No man among us is better qualified to counsel us in this regard than our speaker today. Therefore, it is my privilege to present to you ⎯⎯⎯⎯⎯, chief of police/sheriff of our city/county.

Chief of Fire Department

"An ounce of prevention is worth a pound of cure." This old adage is especially applicable to the safety from destructive fires in our businesses and homes. It is for this reason that this week is being observed as "Fire Prevention Week."

Certainly the man among us best qualified to speak on this theme is our speaker today. I take delight, therefore, in presenting to you Chief ⎯⎯⎯⎯⎯ of our city fire department.

61

Minister or Rabbi

The moral and spiritual tone of our community is related directly to its spiritual institutions. And the effectiveness of their influence is measured by the effectiveness of the men who are charged with the leadership of the churches and synagogues. Since our group is concerned with every phase of our community's life, we welcome as our speaker one such leader.

It is unnecessary for me to introduce to you one who is known to each of us either personally or by reputation. Therefore, I do not introduce but present to you the Reverend/Rabbi _____ of the _____ church/synagogue.

DATE DUE			